YOUR KNOWLEDGE HAS VALUE

Daniel Linotte, Khaled Menna

Employment and Unemployment Issues in Algeria

GRIN Verlag

Bibliografische Information der Deutschen Nationalbibliothek:

Die Deutsche Bibliothek verzeichnet diese Publikation in der Deutschen National-
bibliografie; detaillierte bibliografische Daten sind im Internet über http://dnb.d-
nb.de/ abrufbar.

Imprint:

Copyright © 2012 GRIN Verlag GmbH
Druck und Bindung: Books on Demand GmbH, Norderstedt Germany
ISBN: 978-3-656-34482-7

GRIN - Your knowledge has value

Der GRIN Verlag publiziert seit 1998 wissenschaftliche Arbeiten von Studenten, Hochschullehrern und anderen Akademikern als eBook und gedrucktes Buch. Die Verlagswebsite www.grin.com ist die ideale Plattform zur Veröffentlichung von Hausarbeiten, Abschlussarbeiten, wissenschaftlichen Aufsätzen, Dissertationen und Fachbüchern.

Visit us on the internet:

http://www.grin.com/

http://www.facebook.com/grincom

http://www.twitter.com/grin_com

Employment and Unemployment Issues

in

Algeria

St. Anthony's College, Oxford

Centre de Recherche en Economie Appliquée pour le Développement (CREAD), Algiers

(May 2012)

CONTENT

SUMMARY

This short paper concentrates on employment and unemployment issues in Algeria. In a first part, the economic context is presented, from an historical perspective. It underlines that the country's economy relies excessively on hydrocarbons, which contributes to large distortions and has negative impacts on the creation of stable jobs in productive sectors. The second part analyses the labor supply and demand, and the intermediation role of ANEM, the National Employment Agency. Considering labor markets, there is a lack of reliable statistics, the scope and the quality of data on labor supply and demand must definitely be improved. In particular, there is a strong need for a better assessment of the importance of the informal sector, including so-called work at home. Available statistics underline the vulnerability of young generations and women. The role of ANEM is important; however, its performances could still be improved. The third part overviews the roles and impacts of development programs and key-institutions involved in job creation. Here also, improvements are needed. In addition, there is a need for better data and adequate methodology to assess the performance of these institutions.

Introduction

Following the 1986 oil-shock characterized by the collapse of energy prices on world markets, Algeria was confronted with a sharp terms-of-trade deterioration, large trade deficits and a debt crisis. That situation led to drastic adjustments under IMF supervision, a costly process which contributed to very high levels of unemployment, the collapse of living standards, widespread poverty and growing insecurity in the 1990s – a period named Algeria's "dark decade" (or "*décennie noire*" in French).

Thanks to much higher energy prices, the situation improved considerably after 2000. External debts have been eliminated and Algeria presently enjoys fast growing international reserves, amounting to about US$ 200 billion at the beginning of 2012. Such good financial conditions allow the government to spend more money on ambitious development plans, mainly to build new infrastructures and raise social welfare.

Despite improvements, Algeria is still confronted with significant social and economic challenges. The economy relies too much on hydrocarbons and the country could be characterized by the so-called "Dutch disease", the business environment is not seen as conducive, youth unemployment remains quite important, incomes and wealth inequalities seem to be growing, corruption is perceived as very high by domestic and international communities (see for instance Transparency International ratings), governance must be improved.

This paper addresses selected employment and unemployment issues in Algeria. In the first part, the economic context is briefly presented, taking into account the major changes that took place since the country gained independence in 1962. The second part underlines the main features of the supply and demand for labor, including the role of the national employment agency responsible for intermediation on the labor market – the ANEM or "*Agence Nationale de l'Emploi*". Other agencies, policies and measures related to jobs creation (mainly with small businesses) are presented in the third part. Some tentative recommendations are proposed in a last section. Figures and tables are in the Annexes.

1. Economic Context

a. Voluntarism and Economic Development

The central role of planning. After 132 years of French domination and a costly liberation war (1954-1962) in terms of human suffering and loss of lives, Algeria finally became a sovereign state in 1962.[1] Considering social and economic development *per se*, before independence, Algeria was subordinated to the needs of the colonial power – France. The prospects for industrialization were limited and the majority of the Algerian population was *de facto* maintained in extreme poverty and ignorance – with significant levels of underemployment and unemployment – within a system of discrimination.

In 1962, development needs were huge: an entire population must have access to education, health cares and be housed adequately. An "urgency plan" was first adopted in 1962 to develop the labor-intensive textile industry, which should help create thousands of new jobs and provide minimum incomes to the people.

A multiannual development plan was adopted in 1968. Following the Soviet command economy model characterized by central planning and the direct involvement of the state in all spheres of economic activities, Algerian leaders decided to promote a growth and development strategy based on ambitious investment plans and large national companies financed by the revenues of oil and gas exports.

---

[1] According to scholars, the two first decades of French colonization led to a collapse of the domestic population, from 4 million in 1830 to 2.7 million twenty years after, a loss of more than 30% – genocide-like figures. It will take more than 80 years for France to control all Algerian territories. Thus, the Touareg tribes of the Southern part of Sahara will be defeated after WWI only.

"Industrializing industries". The President of Algeria Houari Boumediene insisted on "rapid, massive and comprehensive" industrialization. In addition to Soviet influence, the key-concepts that supported that strategy were also based on the work of the French economist Gérard Destanne de Bernis from Grenoble University; he was a strong supporter of the independence of French colonies and developed the idea of "industrializing industries" (*"industries industrialisantes"*) or industries that are expected to promote other activities with the production of intermediates and final goods, for consumption and investment (Boudjenah, 2002, page 65).[2] From a technical perspective, Nobel Prize winner Leontieff's input-output tables may allow the identification of forward and backward linkages among industries and help identify the best ones for fast GDP growth.

Considering economic sectors or industries, three priorities were identified:

- Investing heavily in steel and petrochemicals industries because they can rely on the abundant domestic natural resources (iron ore, oil and gas),
- Developing mechanical industries (that can process further steel outputs),
- Imports substitution, in particular for consumption goods.

That strategy required the nationalization of key-sectors and the creation of large companies that will become national monopolies, fully isolated from international competition. In 1969, 49 state-owned companies controlled most of the industrial outputs. The largest company was (and still is) the SONATRACH (the National Company for Research, Production, Processing and Commercialization of Oil and Gas or *"Société Nationale pour la Recherche, la Production, la Transformation et la Commercialisation des Hydrocarbures"*). SONATRACH was created in 1963; it actually represents more than one third of the country GDP, it is one of the largest companies in Africa.

Considering the 1960s international context, Algeria's development strategy was not an exception. Protectionism and import-substitution industrialization (with regional integration among developing

---

[2] Destanne de Bernis was also an innovative follower of another French economist, François Perroux, who developed original views in development economics, giving importance to history, structures and institutions.

nations) were seen as essential by the Argentinian economist Raul Prebisch, the former head of the United Nations Economic Commission for Latin America (better known by its acronym – "CEPAL"), who became the first Secretary General of UNCTAD (1964-1969); he was also one of the Third World fathers of the "structuralist school" and "dependency theory" in the field of development economics.

b. First oil shock, debts and adjustments

1970s euphoria. The oil shock of 1973/74 generated enormous export receipts that permitted to increase substantially the number of investment projects, and acquire modern equipment and fully equipped new plants, or "turnkey factories". During the second four-year plan of 1974-1978, more than 500 medium size enterprises were created, which reinforced and diversified the economic structure of the country.

Limits of a policy. The new development strategy seemed very promising and was even praised in international circles. To some extent, Algeria became a model for economic and social development. However, overall, the industry was lacking competent management and a qualified labor force, new equipment were not fully, efficiently and properly used, productivity and returns were very low, maintenance was rather poor, products were not competitive on international markets.

The restructuring of public enterprises started during the 1980s. There were three major objectives:

- Equipment must be amortized,
- Companies must be made profitable, and
- All loans to companies must be repaid.

The impact of these measures was mitigated because of the excess of economic centralism, a reflection of the mono-party political system. The changes were far too slow and there was no real debate in the country.

Crisis and adjustment. In addition to inefficiencies and wastes, the collapse of oil prices in 1986 led to large macroeconomic imbalances, with the internal and external deficits financed by borrowings on international financial markets and, as a result, the accumulation of debts. The debt crisis worsened rapidly at the beginning of 1994 with a further fall in oil prices and the drying-up of financial resources, which made the request for external assistance unavoidable and a four-year Structural Adjustment Program was finally adopted in May 1994, under strict IMF supervision. In practice, there was first a one-year Standby Arrangement, followed by a three-year Extended Fund Facility.

The reduction of external debts in the 1990s was accompanied by a progressive liberalization of international trade, the reduction of subsidies on basic food products and the beginning of a large scale privatization process. These measures had negative impacts on employment and contributed to the rise of poverty. The labor legislation was also modified to facilitate the mobility of workers and introduce more wage flexibility (Benachenhou and al., 2004). These years of extreme austerity contributed to the climate of civil war.

c. High energy prices and energy rents

New economic growth. Thanks to high energy prices and more favorable terms-of-trade (see Table 1.1), Algeria could adopt the Program to Support Economic Recovery (*"Programme de Soutien à la Relance Economique"*– PSRE) for the period 2001-2004, it was a US$ 5 billion program aiming at the creation of 800.000 jobs.

The US$ 50 billion Plan for the Consolidation of Economic Growth (*"Plan de Consolidation de la Croissance Economique"*) was adopted for the years 2005-2009 to promote all economic sectors and develop infrastructures. It was expected to prepare domestic companies for WTO accession and be confronted with the competition created by the Free Trade Agreement signed with the European Union in 2002, mainly with the adoption of international standards – including "ISO norms" – for domestic products. A 2010-2014 Development Plan is presently implemented.

Nevertheless, the new financial bonuses mean that the country does not need external assistance. The (rather slow) path of liberalization seems to be questioned by domestic economic and political circles. Eventually, one result of the new financial conditions could be the restriction imposed on foreign investors by a law adopted in 2009 which limits to 49% foreign participation in new companies. Such a policy is partly justified by the need to address seemingly growing capital outflows generated by FDIs and better promote the transfer of technology and competences. There could even be a new wave of import substitution measures.

Economic distortions and social challenges. Despite costly attempts to diversify the domestic economy and exports, economic development in Algeria continues to rely heavily on the energy sector – oil and gas (see Box 1.1). The country could be confronted with a variety of the so-called "Dutch Disease", which happens when for various reasons a dominant economic activity represents a major obstacle to the development of other sectors. The energy rent could still last for decades (some experts say 50 years), which may constrain the scope for the diversification of the economy and, as a result, not allow the creation of strongly needed thousands of new jobs, especially for the youth.

BOX 1.1: Excessive reliance on hydrocarbons and "Dutch disease" in Algeria – evidence

IMF Survey online: **Could you paint a picture of Algeria's economy today?**

Toujas-Bernaté: The Algerian economy is dominated by oil and gas resources, which account for 98 percent of the country's exports. The hydrocarbon sector represents about 40–45 percent of total GDP and about two-thirds of budget revenues... The country's macroeconomic performance over the past decade has been solid. Because of relatively high oil prices combined with prudent macroeconomic policies, Algeria was able to achieve relatively strong growth, low inflation, and a sharp reduction in public and external debt. It has also accumulated large reserves... That said, major challenges remain – foremost of which is unemployment, which remains high, especially among the youth.

Source: "Algeria Should Reduce Reliance on Oil, Create More Jobs, Says IMF", *IMF Survey online*, January 26, 2011.

A recent study examines the effect of increases of oil price on the key macroeconomic variables of Algeria. Using vectors auto-regression models with linear and non-linear specifications to analyze the data over the period 1995Q1–2007Q3, the findings indicate that the increase in the inflation rate due to oil price shock is the main cause of the real exchange rate's appreciation in the short term, which could be at the origin of the Dutch Disease.

Source: R. Jbir; S. Zouari-Ghorbel, "Oil Price and Dutch Disease: The Case of Algeria", *Energy Sources*, Part B: Economics, Planning, and Policy (June 2011), 6 (3), pg. 280-293.

2. Evolution of employment and unemployment in Algeria

a. Supply of labor

"Demographic transition?" The dynamic and the structure of the total population influence the supply of labor in a country. Following independence, Algeria has been confronted with a demographic explosion; the total population increased four times, from 9 million in 1962 to 37 million in 2012. Moreover, fertility and population growth rates decreased during the 1980s and the 1990s (see Table 2.1), phenomena that were seen as positive for the development of the country; it was explained by various factors: higher levels of education for boys and girls, family planning measures, urbanization, housing problems and insecurity during the 1990s, etc.

It seemed that the country was going to complete a full "demographic transition" (see Box 2.1 for an explanation), which would definitely reduce pressures on the labor market. In fact, the population growth rate increased after 2000. This acceleration could be caused by the growing number of marriages and rising birth rates, which are themselves determined by better living conditions and more security in the country; more traditional behaviors could also contribute to these changes.

BOX 2.1: Demographic transition

The idea of demographic transition is mainly based on the work of the American demographer W. Thompson (1887–1973). The population growth rate of most societies would go through four (or five) different stages: 1) **stagnation** – preindustrial societies are characterized by high levels of death and birth rates, and overall, population stagnates; 2) **acceleration** – in the second stage, following scientific progress, higher food supply and better living conditions, the death rate decreases and the birth rate remains high, as a result, the population growth rate accelerates; 3) **deceleration** – the death rate is low and the birth rate decreases, population growth decelerates; 4) **stabilization** – the death and the birth rates are both low, population stabilizes… this would correspond to a mature society; 5) **decline** – a fifth stage is sometime considered, with very low fertility and birth rates and a declining population.

Most developing countries are in stage 2 or 3; most developed countries are in stage 3 or 4. Germany and Russia are confronted with significant demographic declines, which correspond to stage 5. French, Belgian and Polish populations still grow, etc. Considering Algeria, since 2000, the population growth rate accelerates. De facto, the four/five stages population theory (or demographic transition) is not fully supported by data.

Labor force. According to official statistics, with the exception of 1990, 2000 and 2007, the labor force (actually employed and unemployed) grew continuously in Algeria since 1980. It reached 10.81 million in September 2010, of which 9.73 million were actually employed. It corresponded to an occupation rate of 27.2% (i.e. the share of labor force in the total population above 14). In 2010, women represented only 15.1% of the employed labor force.

The dynamic of unemployment. The macroeconomic adjustments imposed during the "dark decade" (the 1990s) severely impacted on the rate of unemployment that reached a maximum of 30% in 2000. After that historical peak, the unemployment rate decreased to reach a low 9.9% at the end 2010 (see Table 2.1). Despite significant improvements on the labor market, the unemployment figures provided by official statistics raise questions. For instance, when considering labor force data reported in an IMF report published in 2008, the absolute decline of unemployment in 2004 corresponds exactly to additional work at home, which is a category that belongs mainly to the informal sector – a rather odd finding indeed (see Annex 2 for more information).

Gender dimensions. More and more women are looking for paid jobs; they want to join the labor force and they also contribute to unemployment. Women participation in the labor force is above all an urban phenomenon and reflects new attitudes and changing behaviors, which is explained by higher levels of education, the 1990s crisis and its impacts on household incomes and living conditions, and a growing number of divorces. Nevertheless, the participation rates of women are still far below those of men and their unemployment rate is more than twice higher what is observed for men: 19.1% versus 8.1% in 2010. Furthermore, figures provided for 2005 and 2010 in Table 2.2 show that the gap does not decrease overtime, on the contrary.

The higher unemployment rate that is observed for women could reflect the absence of equal treatment between men and women on the labor market – in fact, gender discrimination is often reported despite anti-discrimination domestic laws and the signing of gender equality international conventions by Algeria, in particular Convention 111 of the International Labor Office, ILO.

Youth unemployment. The age structure of the unemployed underlines youth vulnerability. In 2010, youth (with an age in the range 14-24) unemployment reached 21.5%, which is three times higher than the corresponding rate observed for adult generations (with an age above 24). Here also, the situation does not improve overtime. For young women, the unemployment rate reached 37.6% in 2010, which is twice higher than what is observed for young men.

Education and unemployment. The highest rates of unemployment are observed for those who have obtained diplomas from the higher education system; graduate unemployment reached 20.3% in 2010 versus 1.9% for those who have no education at all. For graduate women, the rate of unemployment is three times higher than what is observed for men. These features are quite resilient and correspond to a tremendous waste of human resources and public money. Highly qualified people also try to emigrate to countries where they can find adequate jobs – Algeria is *de facto* confronted with a brain drain process which benefits to richer countries, in Europe and elsewhere.

Children at work. Recent student studies indicate that thousands of children do work, most often for little money and without much legal protection. According to the result of a census completed in 2001, one million workers started working before 16; these workers represented 16% of the total active labor force. In the Algiers wilaya (province), there were 330.000 children at work. In the city of Algiers alone, one fifth of the children could "escape" from compulsory education – a worrying situation (for details, see Musette, 2006).

Retirement and work. Many retired workers do work in Algeria. This is explained by various factors. Thus, low retirement benefits do not always allow the satisfaction of basic needs, especially in remote regions where geographical conditions may require a minimum of self-sufficiency activity. In urban areas, public administrations and private companies employ highly qualified and experienced officially retired persons. It should be noted that full pensions are already paid after 10-15 years of full time work in a managerial position in public administration, which could represent a stimulus for early retirement and the search for other well-paid jobs – it could also explain the lack of motivation at work and the relative absence of individuals' initiative in the public administration. Maintaining a minimum of economic activities is also a way to avoid "social death".

Explaining unemployment. An explanation of unemployment in Algeria is proposed by an IMF study. Algeria is compared to MENA (Middle Eastern and North African countries). That study underlines the very low productivity of Algerian companies. The legal and administrative environment, including pervasive corruption and complex procedures, is not business conducive for both actual and potential foreign investors and domestic entrepreneurs (Kpodar, 2007).

b. Demand for labor

The importance of the informal sector. The informal sector can be found in many activities: agriculture, services (retail trade, transport of people and commodities…), even in well-known large public and private companies which might not be willing to declare all their workers for cost reasons, in particular to avoid compulsory financial contributions to social security. De facto, the border line between informal and formal sectors is thin.

Considering available data, the informal sector grew since the 1990s and could represent more than one third of total employment (see Table 2.3). As also indicated by table A2.1, 49.4% of employment growth between 2002 and 2006 would correspond to work at home, a category that belongs mainly to the informal sector. A study conducted in 2007 and based on a sample of 522 households living in Bejaïa, a coastal city located 280 km east of Algiers, young workers (below 30) tend to work first in the informal sector as employees. Older workers (40+) generally work in the formal sector. The workers who are 30-40 belong to both informal and formal sectors. In other words, the more mature the workers, the more they seem ready to legalize their job status. The same study shows that 63.5% of the workers employed in the non-agricultural private sectors are not officially recorded, a proportion that is lower than what is reported for 2007 by the National Office of Statistics, namely 72.7% (see

Bellache, 2011; ONS, 2008). In addition, as shown in Table 2.3, the importance of the informal sector does not decline overtime.

"Booming manufacturing?" There were about half-a-million workers employed in manufacturing in 1999 (see Table 2.4). Such a low figure underlines the failure of industrialization policies initiated in the 1960s and 1970s, after gaining independence. Considering more recent years, manufacturing was the fastest growing sector over the period 1999-2010. Thus, in 2010, employment in manufacturing reached 1.3 million, 2.7 times higher than in 1999 – a surprising finding that may raise methodological questions about data.

The new legislation on FDIs, requiring joint ventures between nationals and foreign partners, with minority participation for foreigners, could eventually help boost domestic entrepreneurship and, as a result, contribute to jobs creation in manufacturing. Nevertheless, foreign investments contribute to the transfer of technology and competences.

The construction sector. The energy rent helps finance the construction of new infrastructures, office buildings and housing, which contributes to the creation of new jobs.

The East-West Motorway, of a length of 1216 km, was one of the biggest state-financed projects. Chinese and Japanese companies won the bids for that project. They promised to train Algerian workers and provide jobs for local people. However, foreigners were actually employed in these activities that do not seem very attractive for domestic workers – the large presence of Chinese workers in specific urban areas also created tensions with the local population and the training of the local labor force was rather disappointing.

Trade - services - public administration. This is the largest sector in terms of employment, which reflects the importance of the state apparatus in the country. In 2010, 34.4% of the population worked in the public sector, where they can directly benefit from energy rent bonuses.

c.   The intermediation role of ANEM

A central agent on the labor market. The National Employment Agency (ANEM) – which is controlled by the Ministry of Labor, Employment and Social Security – is a new institution; it was created in 2006 to replace the ONAMO (National Office of the Labor Force or *Office National de la Main d'Oeuvre*). ANEM has hundreds of agencies; it is a four-level structure - national, regional, provincial and local. According to the law, all job seekers and employers must use the services of ANEM (or other legally authorized entities).

De facto, ANEM is the main official intermediate on the labor market, between those who are actively looking for jobs (which corresponds to the labor supply) and potential employers, private or public (namely the labor demand). Considering Table 2.5, about 20% of job seekers can find a job through ANEM. In addition, a quarter of offered jobs through ANEM could not be matched in 2007.

ANEM performances. Overall, when considering the demand for jobs by those who are unemployed, the rate of successful placement (i.e. when there is effective intermediation through ANEM) remains low – nevertheless it should be noted that matching is constrained by the supply of jobs, not ANEM *per se*. In addition, many jobs offered by employers are not filled by the agency.

Most registered job seekers are new on labor markets and, according the recent labor surveys, ANEM covers only a limited segment of these markets. In fact, most jobs are found without ANEM. In the Algerian context (and in many other countries also), personal relations and luck do matter a lot to find jobs. Such a situation requires innovative actions to create more jobs with new enterprises and better satisfy the requirements of offered jobs with adequate education and training. To some extent, the actual situation could change in a near future, thus ANEM benefits from international technical assistance projects that are expected to strengthen its role on labor markets.

d. Labor market flexibility

Employment-GDP elasticities. A recent IMF study (see P. Furceri, 2012) shows that the employment-non hydrocarbon GDP elasticity is rather high: 0.64 for the reference period. However, there are significant differences between young and adult workers: "differentiating between the age group 15–24 and the group aged 24+ ... the (arc) elasticity for young people over the recent 5 years has been half of the average (arc) elasticity for total employment and about one third of the arc elasticity of the age group 24+" (page 5). In other words, economic growth does not create strongly needed jobs for the youth and there is *de facto* age discrimination, which may have negative impacts on the social climate.

International comparisons. IMF experts also measure labor market flexibility in Algeria and other comparable countries. Algerian labor markets are significantly less flexible than those of other MENA and emerging countries. Moreover, labor market flexibility decreases overtime, which means growing rigidities on labor markets. Such findings could indicate that the liberalization process has slowed down in Algeria, which may have consequences on the competitiveness of the domestic economy and job creation in the long run, especially for the youth.

3. Employment policies and related institutions

a. Macroeconomic programs

As mentioned in section 1, since 2000, two large scale programs have already been completed to promote development, growth and employment. A third plan is currently implemented.

The 2001-2004 Program to Support Economic Recovery. It promoted labor-intensive activities with the construction of public infrastructures in remote rural and mountainous regions, the highlands and the south (Sahara). It was expected to create 850.000 jobs, more than 200.000 per year, of which 80%

should be permanent ones. The impacts of that program are seen as modest by the National Economic and Social Committee (CNES – *Comité National Economique et Social*, an autonomous public body that evaluates policies and advise the government). According to the CNES, the plan contribution to GDP growth was limited to 1%, which represented only one seventh of the GDP average growth rate of 6.9% for the reference period. A more positive assessment underlines that 457.431 new jobs were created in 16 months, from September 2001 till December 2002 (Musette and al., 2003, page 51).

The 2005-2009 Economic Growth Consolidation Plan. Originally, it was a US$ 50 billion plan that became a US$ 280 billion plan, of which 150 billion were finally spent. From the beginning, there were criticisms. Some analysts indicated that it does not really address structural problems, it was definitely not long term oriented. For instance, when large scale projects (e.g. motorways) were completed, most related jobs just disappeared. Furthermore, thousands of foreigners were employed full time for many years in these projects. In addition, important issues such as industrial restructuring and the development of competitive services (banking, insurances, tourism, transports...) were not addressed and a more comprehensive and viable economic base must still be established in the country, beside the energy sector.

The 2010-2014 Development Plan. The actual Plan mobilizes US$ 286 billion; it is expected to create 3 million additional jobs and 40.000 micro-companies, mainly through two key-institutions: ANSEJ and CNAC (see hereafter).

b. SMEs promotion institutions

Three key-institutions. In addition to ANEM, three major institutions, under the authority of the Ministry of Labor, Employment and Social Security, were created to contribute to the reduction of unemployment and promote employment with new small and medium enterprises (SMEs):

- The National Fund for Unemployment Insurance (*"Caiisse Nationale d'Assurance Chômage"* – CNAC),

- The National Agency to Support Youth Employment (or *"Agence Nationale de Soutien à l'Emploi des Jeunes"* – ANSEJ) and

- The National Agency for Micro-loans Management (*"Agence Nationale de Gestion du Microcrédit"* – ANGEM).

ANSEJ. Since its creation in 1997, ANSEJ provides micro-loans to support youth entrepreneurship (from the age of 19 till 35, exceptionally till 40); until recently, these loans could reach the equivalent of *circa* US$ 135.000, with 10-20% self-funding. According to official sources, 170.000 micro-firms and 500.000 jobs have been promoted with the aid of ANSEJ between 1997 and 2011, with a rather low rate of failure - namely 3%. In 2011 alone, 42.000 projects were accepted, which led to the creation of 98.000 new jobs – overall, one ANSEJ project corresponds to 2.5-3 work places, mainly in the service sector.

The critiques of ANSEJ underline the lack of assistance to prepare project proposals and support their realization. Women led projects represent only a small share of all funded projects, which is in line with their low participation in the labor force. Procedures are slow and time consuming for applicants. Even when a project is accepted, it takes much time to obtain loans from public banks. Abuses and fraud have been reported; for instance, well established businessmen use ANSEJ indirectly by hiring the services of young entrepreneurs. Data about ANSEJ activities are also controversial (see Boukrif et Bellataf, no date).

Despite negative comments, it should be noted that in a near future ANSEJ will initiate four-days training courses for young entrepreneurs to better prepare them to administrative tasks related to accounting, taxation, social security and the set of regulations and procedures for public procurements; these courses should reduce bankruptcy risks. Companies that are confronted will financial difficulties will receive more attention and support. In addition, the rate of self-financing will decrease to reach a low 1-2% symbolic level.

ANGEM. Following its creation in 2004, ANGEM supported the development of work at home with small (revolving) loans, often below 50 dollars until recently. Such small loans do allow to buy small quantities of raw materials that will be processed and then sold. At the end of 2011, after 6 years of operations, 275.000 loans had been supplied, contributing to the creation of 400.000 jobs. In February 2011, it was decided to increase the value of loans available for raw material and equipment. Most of the activities funded by ANGEM seem to belong to the informal sector and women represent the majority of the borrowers; considering reimbursement, women are also seen as less risky than men.

CNAC. That institution was created in 1994 to address unemployment caused by the closure of public enterprises within the framework of the Structural Adjustment Program – SAP. CNAC helps the unemployed workers to create their own enterprises; their age must be in the range 35-50. Funds are financed by the compulsory contributions to the unemployment insurance. Here also, the reality is complex. Until recently, at least 14 procedures were needed to start a company. Financial conditions are seen as very strict and the banking system seems to be lacking flexibility when entrepreneurs are confronted with extreme or exceptional difficulties. Nevertheless, measures were adopted in 2011 to ease procedures.

      c.   Evaluating and comparing actions

Table 3.1 reports evaluations of the costs of jobs created by ANJEM, ANGEM and the PSR. ANJEM seems to perform better than the PSR. Nevertheless, there are quite large discrepancies between evaluations. Moreover, bankruptcies may not be properly recorded and many loans are simply not reimbursed, borrowers may even just disappear – how is that taken into account? Considering the PSR, not all created jobs are permanent, etc.

<u>Final remarks</u>

Following 50 years of independence and despite a huge territory with a unique endowment in natural resources, Algeria is still confronted with major social and economic challenges – some of them relate directly or indirectly to labor markets, employment and unemployment:

i.   The country's economy relies excessively on hydrocarbons, which contributes to large economic distortions, including the "Dutch Disease" and subsequent negative impacts on the creation of stable jobs in productive sectors.

ii.   Considering labor markets, there is a lack of reliable statistics, the scope and the quality of data on labor supply and demand must be improved.

iii.   In particular, there is a need for a better assessment of the importance of the informal sector, including so-called work at home.

iv.   The acceleration of population growth after 2000 could have important consequences on social needs and the labor market in the long run.

v.   The high rate of youth unemployment must be reduced with the better use of exiting instruments and new ones, focusing above all on the promotion of new businesses for which basic training, monitoring and adequate support is essential – ANSEJ, ANGEM and CNAC should continue to play leading roles to promote such businesses.

vi.   Gender-related dimensions of employment and unemployment must be addressed adequately.

vii. ANEM performances must definitely improve. For that purpose, it must be fully integrated with the other institutions that have an impact on labor supply and demand – ANSEJ, ANGEM, CNAC, business associations, training and education bodies, at all levels.

viii. A few years ago, children at work are another source of concerns; there is a need to assess the present situation.

ix. The evaluation of the performances of past and actual job creation programs and institutions must be based on adequate statistics and internationally recognized standards.

x. Considering Algeria's growing financial resources, optimism should prevail, especially if efforts are made to improve the quality of governance of public bodies involved on labor markets.

References

AFP (3 novembre 2008), « Algérie : le projet de révision de la Constitution renforce l'exécutif ».

ANEM – Agence Nationale de l'Emploi (Algeria), yearly and quarterly statistical data on the labor markets, unpublished, various years and quarters.

Y. Bellache, *L'économie informelle en Algérie, une approche par enquête auprès des ménages – le cas de Bajaia*. Thèse de Doctorat. En cotutelle. University of Bejaia (Algeria) and Paris-Est Créteil (France), version 1 – 17 May 2011. On the web.

A. Benachenhou et al. (2004), *Du Budget au Marché*, Alpha Editions, Alger.

A. Benyahia (19 septembre 2004), « Plan de Consolidation de la Croissance : 50 milliards de dollars et des questions », *El Watan*, Alger.

Y. Boudjenah (2002), *Algérie : décomposition d'une industrie : la restructuration des entreprises publiques (1980-2000) : l'Etat en question*, L'Harmattan.

M. Boukrif et M. Bellataf (pas de date), « Politique algérienne d'insertion des jeunes : entre la logique économique et la vision sociale », on the web.

G. Destanne de Bernis (1966), « Industries industrialisantes et contenu d'une politique d'intégration régionale », *Economie Appliquée*, no 3-4.

D. Furceri (April 2012), "Unemployment and Labor Market Issues in Algeria", IMF Working Papers, WP/12/99.

A. Hadj-Nacer (2011), *La Martingale Algérienne*, Barzakh Editions, Algiers.

IMF (March 2008 ; 1), *Algeria: Statistical Appendix*, IMF Country Report No. 08/102.

IMF (March 2008 ; 2), *Algeria : 2007 Article IV Consultation – Staff Report ; Public Information Notice on the Executive Board Discussion ; and Statement by the Executive Director for Algeria*, IMF Country Report 08/103.

IMF (January 26, 2011), "Algeria Should Reduce Reliance on Oil, Create More Jobs, Says IMF", IMF Survey online.

L. Kachemad (February 21, 2012), "Ghardaïa: L'ANSEJ dresse son bilan 2011", *Liberté*, Algiers.

R. Jbir and S. Zouari-Ghorbel (2011), "Oil Price and Dutch Disease: The Case of Algeria", *Energy Sources*, Part B: Economics, Planning, and Policy, June, 6 (3), pg. 280-293.

K. Kpodar (2007), « Why Has Unemployment in Algeria Been Higher than in MENA and Transition Countries? », IMF Working Paper 07/210.

A. Mokaddem, D. Linotte et R. Chalal, *Problèmes de l'Emploi et du Chômage en Algérie*, 2009.

S. Mouhoudi (2009), *Les vulnérabilités – Cas de l'Algérie*, ENAG Editions, Algiers.

M. S. Musette, M. A. Isli et N. E. Hammouda (2003), *Marché du Travail et Emploi en Algérie – Eléments pour une Politique Nationale de l'Emploi*, OIT, Alger.

M. S. Musette (2006), « Le travail des enfants en Algérie », dans : *Paupérisation des Sociétés Maghrébines*, MS Musette (éd), Reflet de l'économie sociale, CREAD, Alger, pp 117-149.

ONS/Office National de Statistiques (2008), *Enquête emploi auprès des ménages (2007)*.

M. Rabhi (21 février 2005), « Corruption : le FMI épingle l'Algérie », *Liberté*.

Z. Riabi (2006), « Communication au séminaire final pour l'année 2006 du groupe Méda ETE – Cadre Nationaux de Certification », Ministère de la Formation et de l'Enseignement Professionnel, République Algérienne Démocratique et Populaire, Le Caire, 4 et 5 décembre.

G. Sensenbrenner et B. Loko (mars 2008), « Estimating the Equilibrium Real Exchange Rate in Algeria », dans : *Algeria : selected issues*, IMF country report No. 8/104.

Yazid Taled (March 21, 2011), "Algérie: l'emploi des jeunes, combien ça coûte", *Le Quotidien d'Oran*, Tags : Algérie Emploi Jeunesse.

Websites

National Office of Statistics (Office National de Statistics – ONS), Algeria: www.ons.dz.

National Employment Agency (Agence Nationale de l'Emploi - ANEM), Algeria: www.anem.dz.

ANNEX 1: Tables and Figures

Table 1.1: Algeria – Selected economic indicators, 2002-2010

Indicators	2002	2003	2004	2005	2006	2007	2008	2009	2010
Real GDP (GR, in %)	4.7	6.9	5.2	5.1	2.0	6.3	6.1	9.3	5.9
Real non-hydrocarbon GDP (GR, %)	5.3	6.0	6.2	4.7	5.6	7.3	15.4	-9.9	16.3
Consumer price index (GR, %)	1.4	2.6	3.6	1.6	2.5	3.5	4.5	5.7	3.9
Terms of Trade (GR, %) (1)	-8.6	9.7	13.6	30.0	9.8	0.8	22.5	-26.8	22.9
Current accounts (% of GDP)	7.6	13.0	13.1	20.7	25.2	22.5	20.1	0.3	7.6
External debts (% of GDP)	39.7	34.3	25.7	16.7	4.9	4.2	3.3	3.8	3.5
GDP per capita (current dollars)	1.819	2.136	2.631	3.122	3.397	3,934	4,962	3,925.9	4,516.3

Sources : IMF (March 2008, 1 et 2 ; January 2012) ; National Statistical Office, Algeria
Notes : GR = growth rate
　　　　(1) Positive values correspond to terms-of-trade improvements

Table 2.1: Algeria - total population; labor force, employed and unemployed (Thousand; rates in %; 1990-2010)

Year	Population		Labor force		Employment		Unemployment	
	'000	Growth Rate	'000	Growth Rate	'000	Growth Rate	'000	Rate
1990	25022	-	5851	-	4695	-	1156	19.8
1991	25643	2.5	6085	4.0	4852	3.3	1233	20.3
1992	26271	2.4	6318	3.8	4974	2.6	1344	21.3
1993	26894	2.4	6561	3.8	5042	1.4	1519	23.2
1994	27496	2.2	6814	3.9	5154	2.2	1660	24.4
1995	28060	2.1	7561	11.0	5436	5.5	2125	28.1
1996	28566	1.8	7811	3.3	5625	3.5	2186	28.0
1997	29045	1.7	7918	1.5	5708	1.5	2210	27.9
1998	29507	1.6	8326	5.2	5993	5.0	2333	28.0
1999	29965	1.6	8583	3.1	6073	1.3	2510	29.2
2000	30416	1.5	8154	-5.0	5726	-5.7	2428	29.8
2001	30879	1.5	8568	5.1	6229	8.8	2339	27.3
2002	31357	1.5	8665	1.1	6456	3.6	2209	25.5
2003	31848	1.6	8762	1.1	6684	3.5	2078	23.7
2004	32364	1.6	9470	8.1	7798	16.7	1672	17.7
2005	32906	1.7	9492	0.2	8044	3.2	1448	15.3
2006	33481	1.7	10110	6.6	8869	10.3	1241	12.3
2007	34096	1.8	9968	-1.4	8594	-3.1	1374	13.8
2008	34591	1.4	10315	3.4	9146	6.4	1169	11.3
2009	35268	1.9	10544	2.2	9472	3.5	1072	10.1
2010	35978	2.0	10812	2.5	9735	2.7	1077	9.9

Source: National Office of Statistics, Algeria
Note: Data are not fully comparable overtime

Table 2.2: Algeria - gender, age and education aspects of unemployment (Unemployment rates, in %; 2005 and 2010)

GENDER			
	Female	*Male*	Female/male
2005	17.5	14.8	1.18
2010	19.1	8.1	2.3
AGE			
	Youth (16-24)	*Adult (25+)*	Youth/adult
2005	31.1	10.4	3.0
2010	21.5	7.1	3.0
EDUCATION			
	Higher education - HE	*No education – NE*	HE/NE
2010	21.4	7.3	2.9

Source: National Office of Statistics, Algeria
Note: Data are not fully comparable overtime

Tableau 2.3: Estimates of employment in the informal economy in Algeria (Thousands; share in non-agricultural employment, %)

Year	Minimum		Maximum	
	Total	Share	Total	Share
1985		25.6		
1992	776	18.2	1657	38.9
1997	572	12.3	1991	42.7
2001	1080	22.8	2266	47.7
2007		29.4		43.8

Source : M. S. Musette éd. (2003), p. 49 ; Y. Bellache (2010), p. 79

Table 2.4: Sectorial evolution of employment in Algeria (1999 and 2010)

Sectors	1999		2010		
	'000	%	'000	%	Index
Agriculture	1185	19.5	1136	11.7	96
Manufacturing	493	8.1	1337	13.7	271
Infrastructures and construction	743	12.2	1886	19.4	253
Trade - services - administration	2477	40.8	5377	55.2	217
Work at home	1175	19.4			
Total	6073	100.0	9735	100	160

Source: National Statistical Office of Algeria
Note: For the index, 1999 = 100

Table 2.5: ANEM and ONAMO - Jobs demanded and offered and placement (2003-2007)

Années	Demand - D	Offer - O	Placement - P	O/D %	P/O %	P/D %
2003	234093	47057	39205	20,1	83,3	16,7
2004	570736	73317	57046	12,8	77,8	10,0
2005	505287	86067	64092	17,0	74,5	12,7
2006	712136	132117	96850	18,6	73,3	13,6
2007	887097	168950	125641	19,0	74,4	14,1

Source : National Employment Agency (Agence National de l'Emploi - ANEM), Algeria.

Table 3.1: Comparison of jobs creation costs in Algeria – ANSEJ, ANGEM and PSR

Institution/ Program	Method of calculation	Cost of creation of one job (DA)	Sources/ Remarks
ANSEJ	Total cost of planned investment/total number of jobs to be created	1,123,540	Musette and al. (2003), p. 33
		611,618	Estimate provided by the Ministry of Finance, end of 2004
ANSEJ, Willaya of Gardhai, 2011	Total cost/number of jobs created 1418 direct jobs were created; the total cost is DA 489 millions	350,000	Estimate based on L. Kachemad (February 21, 2012)
ANSEJ + ANGEM (+ other job creation mechanisms?)	Total cost/number of jobs created ANSEJ: total number of permanent jobs created since beginning of activities = 400,000 ANJEM: number of microloans since beginning of activities = 190,000; it is assumed that these loans corresponded to 300,000 jobs (nevertheless, this correspond to a 6-year period; therefore, we assume that 100,000 permanent jobs might have been created, a rough estimate indeed) ANSEJ + ANJEM = 500,000 jobs Total cost: DA 230 billion	460,000	Very rough estimate based on Yazid Taled (March 21, 2011)
Program to Support Economic Recovery/ Programme de Soutien à la Relance, PSR	Estimate based on the cost of major infrastructures in the Program/total number of permanent jobs to be created	2,047,665	Musette and al. (2003), p. 33
	Total cost of the Program/total number of permanent and temporary jobs to be created	846,061	Calculations based on Musette and al. (2003), p. 50

ANNEX 2

Work at home and unemployment changes in Algeria – IMF data

Table A2.1: Active labor force, employment and unemployment in Algeria
(Thousands, 2002-2006)

Year	Active labor force	Employment				Unemployment
		Total	Agriculture	Other sectors	Work at home	
2002	9305	6917	1438	4024	1455	2388
2003	9540	7278	1565	4176	1537	2262
2004	9780	8051	1617	4364	2070	1729
2005	10027	8497	1683	4539	2275	1530
2006	10267	9002	1780	4737	2485	1265

Source : FMI (mars 2008 ; 1)

Considering labor market statistics reported by the IMF, the interpretation of unemployment figures is difficult. Thus, work at home grew faster than other categories of employment - and work at home belongs mainly to the informal sector.

In addition, in 2004, the reduction of unemployment does correspond exactly to the increase of work at home, namely 533.000 – an odd result indeed.

Moreover, despite the limited number of reference data, correlation coefficients between:
- the annual variations of employment in agriculture, non-agricultural sectors and work at home, and
- the annual variations of unemployment,
underline that there is:
1) a low positive correlation between unemployment and employment in agriculture,
2) an absence of significant correlation between unemployment and non-agricultural employment,
3) a strong negative correlation between unemployment and work at home.

Table A2.2: correlation coefficient CORR between the annual changes of
unemployment and employment categories

Parameters	Agricultural employment	Non agricultural employment	Work at Home
CORR	0,75	-0,51	-0,99
T-stat	0,98	-0,55	-2,63
P-value	0,16	0,28	0,004
Comment	Weak positive correlation	Non significative Correlation	Strong negative Corrélation

Authors' bio:

Dr. Daniel Linotte is senior associate member at St. Anthony's College (Oxford). He is consultant in the field of international, transition and development economics, social and labor policies, and security-related economic and environmental issues. He worked as a team leader and senior expert in technical assistance and cooperation projects in the former USSR, the Balkans, South East Asia, the Middle East, North and Sub-Saharan Africa. He also worked for international organizations (including the Council of Europe, OSCE, OECD, UNECE, UNIDO and UNCTAD) and held teaching positions in the US, the EU and Russia. He published articles and books on transition and development economics, international trade, social conditions and sustainable development.

Dr. Khaled Menna is research fellow in CREAD (Centre de Recherche en Economie Appliquée pour le Développement), Algiers. He wrote articles on development, banking and macroeconomic issues in Algeria. He also taught international economics.